DOUBLE TRAITORS?

'—Damnation!—
Only in destroying I
find ease
to my re-
lentless
thoughts.'

PORTRAIT

OF A

SOLDIER YEOMAN.

[TAKEN FROM LIFE.]

HISTORY.

I AM one of the glorious creatures of the opposer of the brethren, descended of *noble* parents from an ancient family of Tinkers, famous for their skill in coining, as well, as their many glorious exploits of robbery, house-breaking and heroic murder;—my great-grand-father minced for betraying his Country—my grand-father danced before the Sheriff for a Rape—my grand-mother hamstrung for her activity at sucking cows—my uncle and aunt roasted for crim-con. together—my father after breaking a house and ripping a woman with child, fell on his way home with the booty, and died shortly after of the accident— my mother scourged for shop-lifting, and afterwards drummed-a-regiment—myself twice tryed for my love of mutton, and once for beef—assisted the woman to *send home* my child—whittled my brother—assaulted a *gentleman*, to expiate for which I am now become a LEGALLY *sworn Murderer*—a gallant *YEOMAN !!!*

DOUBLE TRAITORS?

THE BELFAST VOLUNTEERS AND YEOMEN

1778–1828

A. BLACKSTOCK

THE BELFAST SOCIETY
IN ASSOCIATION WITH
THE ULSTER HISTORICAL FOUNDATION

First published 2000
by the Belfast Society, c/o Linen Hall Library,
17 Donegall Square North, Belfast BT1 5GD
in association with the Ulster Historical Foundation
12 College Square East, Belfast, BT1 6DD

Distributed by
the Ulster Historical Foundation

© Allan Blackstock
ISBN 0-9539604-1-2

Printed by the Northern Whig
Design by Dunbar Design

ACKNOWLEDGEMENTS

I would like to thank the following individuals and institutions for permission to draw on material in their keeping: The Deputy Keeper of the Records, PRONI; Mrs Cottam; Mr Michael Duffin; Dr G. Haslett Connor; Viscount Massereene and Ferrard; Major J.R. Perceval Maxwell; the Linen Hall Library; the National Library of Ireland; the National Archives of Ireland; the British Library; the Royal Irish Academy; Trinity College, Dublin. The Home Office Papers are Crown copyright.

Samuel Neilson, 1761–1803,
woollen draper, United Irishman and editor of the *Northern Star*

DOUBLE TRAITORS?

THE BELFAST VOLUNTEERS AND YEOMEN
1778–1828

TWO DAYS AFTER THE Battle of Ballynahinch on 13 June 1798, Lord Downshire's agent, Thomas Lane, sent his lordship a significant report. Lane told Downshire that the Hillsborough Yeomen, who had been 'scouring' the countryside, had captured the United Irishmen's leader Henry Munro. They also brought in 'many cartloads of pikes … and some of the Castle guns which were found on the field of battle'.[1] The immediate connection between the two finds was too obvious to be stated. So was the consequence, which saw Munro's execution several days later and the subsequent display of his severed head on a pike from Lisburn Market House. However there was another connection between the defeated general and the discarded arms of his broken army, which stretched back years beyond 1798 and indeed beyond the formation of the first United Irish societies in the autumn of 1791. This connection was the Irish Volunteers, local corps raised, independently of government, to defend the country during the troop shortages of the American War of 1775–83. The unfortunate Munro had been a member of the Lambeg Volunteers and many of the 'Castle guns' were muskets which, in 1778–9, had been given by the government to the Irish Volunteers. Munro was not unusual in having a Volunteering background. Many of the most famous northern United Irishmen had once been Volunteers, including William Drennan, Robert Simms, William Sinclair, William Tennant, Samuel Neilson, Steel Dickson, Jemmy Hope and Henry Joy McCracken. Indeed McCracken's artillery at the battle of Antrim consisted of a cannon, which had once belonged to the Templepatrick Volunteers.[2] In this light, there seem good grounds to claim that the

Volunteering activity of the 1780s had its dénouement in 1798.

In 1828 however, when one of the most prominent northern United Irishmen, Charles Hamilton Teeling of Lisburn, wrote his account of the '98 rising, though he praised the original Volunteers of 1782, he went on to note that some had reneged on their traditions of independence and actually joined the government's yeomanry force[3] which fought the United men in 1798. Teeling excoriates these people, scathingly dubbing them 'double traitors' because, in his eyes, they had forsaken their Volunteering and possibly even United Irish past, to oppose their own countrymen.[4] Yet given that the Volunteer-United Irish connection had provided arms, manpower and, in McCracken and Munro, martyrs for the United cause, why, after thirty long years, was Teeling's anger unabated?

Teeling's brutally reductionist analysis suggests that the stances adopted by ex-Volunteers in the years immediately before the rising played an important role in its eventual outcome. It also raises major questions about the nature of Volunteering itself. Although Volunteering had been officially suppressed on the outbreak of war in 1793, many of its former adherents still saw themselves as 'the Volunteers' whether embodied or not, and believed they were the guardians of the movement's traditions of independence. This was particularly the case in the North, and this essay will tackle some of the issues Teeling raises by examining the stances adopted by ex-Volunteers in the events leading up to the rebellion. First, however, we need to know about the Volunteering background.

THE IRISH VOLUNTEERS, 1778–84

Generically, the Volunteers are best seen as part of a long tradition of voluntary military service amongst Irish Protestants which stretched back to the plantations.[5] The conditions for Volunteering were either domestic disturbance or the absence of the garrison of regular soldiers owing to foreign conflict. This contingency was usually met by the embodiment of the militia. When war broke out between Britain and her American Colonies in 1775, the government did not have sufficient money for a militia, and Ireland's defences were left to a very slender regular garrison. However, when France and Spain entered the war and invasion became a possibility in 1778, as there was still no militia, Volunteer corps sprang up spontaneously. The first one was formed in Belfast on Saint Patrick's Day.[6] Although the Protestant self-defence tradition provided a familiar foundation, the Volunteers of the American War period differed in scale and scope from anything that had been seen hitherto. Originally intended to undertake what were known in contemporary parlance as 'police' duties (i.e. peacekeeping by assisting the civil magistrates), they soon became a large-scale national movement wholly independent of government. This movement became known as the Irish Volunteers, or later, in memory of one of their most famous advocates, simply as 'Grattan's Volunteers'. They were an extremely 'democratic' body, in the sense that the normal hierarchical ordering of both civil and military society was subsumed in an organisational system where everyone had a say. The officers held no government commission. Rather, they were either elected from the ranks or from a committee, membership of which was regularly rotated. As indicated by Grattan's famous description of the movement as 'the armed property of the nation',[7] these were men of some substance. In cities and towns they tended to be merchants, tradesmen and professionals, such as lawyers and bankers; in the countryside, they were tenants raised by their landlords. However, whether urban or rural, Volunteers had to be able to afford the cost of their uniforms and equipment and enjoy the luxury of being able to take time off from their regular occupation to train and parade. The muskets alone cost around £1:15:0, not to mention gunpowder at over £4 a barrel for the cheapest grade.[8] They were led by members of the gentry and some clergymen, particularly Presbyterian clergymen in the north.

Apart from drilling and marching, the Volunteers assisted the magistrates who, if requiring additional force, would ordinarily have requested the government to send a detachment of troops. The indications are that Volunteers did this type of duty well. Henry Joy of Belfast, himself an enthusiastic Volunteer, left an unpublished, unfinished history of the Volunteers in which he writes:

> The country at large made greater advances in the first years of the Volunteer institution than it was likely to have done in over a century. The villain could find no screen, nor the laws be trampled on with impunity as the particular knowledge of such numerous bands pledged to the support of order, enabled them to detect every species of criminal without chance of escape.[9]

However the numbers and cohesion of the Volunteer movement, so useful in helping maintain law and order, were soon turned to political purposes.

Because of its radical social implications in these early days, Volunteering was regarded with suspicion by many of Ireland's political elite. However, by 1779, when it became obvious that the government was not going to organise a militia, Volunteering became accepted, indeed respectable. It was endorsed by some of the leading landed magnates, like the Earl of Antrim who, as county governor, gave the Antrim Volunteers the seal of approval by inspecting them and presenting colours. However, the political potential of such a large and well-organised movement was not lost in its new-found 'respectability'. A significant body of 'Patriot' opinion existed within the Irish parliament. These Patriot politicians were men vehemently opposed to the fact that their parliament was subservient to Westminster, which held a veto over Irish legislation. In practical terms the Patriots believed that Britain exercised this power to advance its own interests at the expense of Ireland's, that it lay as a dead hand on Hibernia's trade. Many of these Patriots were themselves involved in Volunteering, and they included men like Henry Grattan, Henry Flood, the Duke of Leinster and the Earl of Charlemont, who became the Volunteers' commander-in-chief, and a powerful relationship soon developed between the Patriots in parliament and the Volunteers outside as a rudimentary political pressure group whose national total now reached around 40,000.[10] This unprecedented and potentially dangerous political liaison showed its colours in 1779 during a demonstration in Dublin against restrictions on Irish trade. Ominously some corps hung placards from the barrels of their cannon demanding 'free trade'. This campaign was successful without the threat of physical force becoming a reality and concessions were achieved. Despite periodic tensions between the Volunteers and the Patriots, the relationship hung together long enough to attain 'legislative independence' for the Irish parliament in 1782.

The means by which this jewel in the crown of Patriot ambition was gained should detain us a while, as, albeit unbeknown to the participants, a myth was being created, which would have reverberations in the 1790s and well beyond. That myth was that Protestants and Catholics united for the independence of their country. It originated in the Presbyterian Meeting House of Dungannon where, on 15 February 1782, a Volunteer Convention was held, attended by delegates from the various companies, to coordinate their demands. Resolutions were passed calling for legislative independence. Included in the 'Dungannon Resolutions' as they became known, was one rejoicing in the relaxation of the penal laws against Catholics.[11] The plan was that these would be adopted by every county Grand Jury, thus presenting the government with a united public opinion, civil and military, Protestant, Catholic and Dissenter, and giving Grattan the moral authority to speak from the floor of the College Green parliament with the voice of the entire Irish people to demand legislative freedom. The British government, under severe domestic pressure fighting an unpopular war, found the demand irresistible and legislative 'independence' – in reality it left much ill-defined – was granted, beginning the period known to generations of 'A' level students as 'Grattan's Parliament'.

VOLUNTEERING IN DECLINE, 1782–89

The winning of legislative independence was the high point of Volunteering. After 1782 the movement split between those, including most of the Patriots, who felt they had what they wanted – more power for the Irish parliament – and those who wanted to reform parliament itself, including many of the northern Presbyterians. Despite the repeal of the Sacramental Test in 1780, Presbyterians were still effectively excluded from a parliament still monopolised by the same class of Anglican landowners as had dominated it throughout the eighteenth century. The reformers embarked on a campaign which, like that for legislative independence, was initiated in Ulster.

In September 1783 another convention of Volunteer delegates was called at Dungannon. These delegates determined to press for a radical programme of reform which included annual parliaments (parliaments could last for up to eight years), voting by secret ballot and the redistribution of parliamentary seats. The key issue of Catholics being given the vote was shelved for decision at a national Volunteer convention to be held at Dublin's Rotunda in November. The attendance at the Dungannon meeting shows the effect the splits were having on northern Volunteering. The solidarity of 1782 was noticeably lacking, as only 278 out of a possible 400 Ulster corps were represented.

Divisions were similarly evident at the Rotunda. Even with the Catholic question left in abeyance, the northern proposals proved too strong for Charlemont, who wanted moderate reform pursued in a moderate manner. After several days of directionless wrangling, a toned down version of the original proposals was produced, which amended the recommendation of annual parliaments in favour of triennial ones, dropped the notion of a secret ballot and completely ignored the Catholic issue. The draft reform bill the Rotunda delegates eventually produced was taken to the College Green parliament by Henry Flood, dressed in full Volunteer regimentals.[12] Not surprisingly the Rotunda proposals were refused point blank by MPs who, in the words of the attorney general, Barry Yelverton, refused to 'register the edicts of another assembly, or to receive proposals at the point of a bayonet.'[13] After this debacle, Volunteering slid into a confused period of deepening internal dissension.

The depth of these divisions can be gauged by the response of different individuals to the Rotunda reform initiative. Charlemont was furious at Flood's behaviour, which he saw as a threatening display of militarism in a constitutional assembly. However, those at the opposite end of the spectrum of Volunteer politics were prepared to go beyond mere military show. William Drennan, the radical Belfast physician and poet, wanted the Volunteers actually to march on the parliament. Napper Tandy, later a famous United Irishman, paraded Volunteer artillery past the parliament house with placards on the cannon which read 'O Lord, open thou our lips, and our mouths shall show forth thy praise'.[14] Further splits appeared over the Catholic issue. Charlemont and Flood wanted it taken off the agenda whereas Frederick Hervey, the sartorially flamboyant and breathtakingly eccentric Earl Bishop of Derry, who had led his Volunteers to the Rotunda in the full regalia of an Anglican bishop, supported Catholic relief to the extent of contemplating an armed uprising to secure it. Indeed Hervey once offered Charlemont the following piece of political strategy: 'We must have blood, my lord, we must have blood!'.[15]

The social composition of Volunteering was also changing. Many of the gentry and middle-class Volunteers left whereas some of the more radical corps began recruiting a new type of member. This began early in 1784, when numbers of working class Catholics were admitted into a corps in the Liberties of Dublin. Charlemont opposed this, but the example was followed elsewhere, prompting Grattan to ask rhetorically in parliament if the 'armed property of the nation' had degenerated to become 'the armed beggary.'[16] However, despite Grattan's hyperbole, the number of enrolled Volunteers in 1784 reflects the movement's continuing overall decline. The government commissioned a secret return which revealed that in Ulster, not only were numbers significantly diminished, but there were actually very few Catholic Volunteers. Although the returns are incomplete – Monaghan and Fermanagh are missing – the total of 7,343 shows that numbers were decimated. At the movement's height in 1782, Ulster had 34,152 Volunteers – the highest total of any province.[17] This decline was again apparent in 1785 when, except for a few corps in Newry and Dublin, there was very limited Volunteer involvement in a petitioning campaign against Pitt's commercial propositions, which the more doctrinaire reformers perceived as diminishing the independence achieved in 1782.[18]

Belfast had been prominent in the heyday of Volunteering. When the foundations of the White Linen Hall were being laid, a glass phial was inserted into the first stone, containing documents praising the Volunteers' role in freeing the long oppressed kingdom of Ireland in 1782.[19] The conditions in the town were tailor-made for political agitation. In the late eighteenth century, Belfast was a growing town with an assertive merchant class who were mainly Presbyterian. Despite the 'victory' of 1782, effective dominance of all political power continued in the hands of a small and unrepresentative group of Anglicans, the nominees of the town's landlord, Lord Donegall. Belfast Volunteers, like the linen merchant William Sinclair, had been prominent in the 1784 reform campaign.[20] However, by 1785, Belfast's radicals began to despair of the Volunteers' political utility as a pressure group. Drennan tried to salvage this by forming an inner circle within the Belfast Volunteers. His idea was to promote a coalition between Dissenter and Catholic to obtain parliamentary reform and thus break the Anglican ascendancy's political monopoly, notions which anticipated those of the United Irishmen six years later. However, the more moderate reformers amongst the remaining Volunteers, headed by Charlemont, were content to channel their energies into Reform Clubs.[21] Here, Volunteering lay stagnating until 1789, when the revolution in France galvanised radicals and reformers in Ireland, as elsewhere, recalling Wordsworth's excited response to the anticipated new era of liberty and freedom:

Bliss was it in that dawn to be alive,
But to be young was very heaven![22]

THE VOLUNTEER REVIVAL, 1790–93

In August 1789 a coalition of opposition MPs formed the Irish Whig Club as a platform for their moderate reforming views. This move was backed by Charlemont, Lord Moira and other powerful aristocratic Whigs. With Charlemont's encouragement, and with an eye open for the forthcoming elections in Antrim and Down,[23] in February 1790 a separate Northern Whig Club was established in Belfast by Alexander Haliday, a medical doctor who had been an officer in the Second Belfast Volunteers and was Charlemont's link with Belfast Volunteering.[24] However, as in 1784, some wanted to go further than others along the reforming road. Middle class Belfast merchants wanted more radical reform than that advocated by Charlemont and the aristocratic Whigs.[25]

Divisions notwithstanding, Haliday and the Northern Whigs decided to organise a parade for 14 July 1791, the second anniversary of the storming of the Bastille, to publicise their political views and give the impression of unity. It was led by the town's two Volunteer corps, followed by Whig Club members decked out in splendid uniforms topped off by green cockades. Large banners and canvasses, redolent with political symbolism, were conveyed through the streets of the town. One canvas, so large it had to be drawn on a cart, depicted Hibernia, the classical figure which represents Ireland, in chains and being released by a Volunteer. In a carefully planned route, the parade covered every important thoroughfare before reaching the White Linen Hall, scene of many previous Volunteer demonstrations. Here, after the obligatory toasts and speechifying, a message of solidarity was sent to France.[26] Arguably though, what Belfast's Bastille celebrations were really about was a struggle between moderates and radicals, both of whom saw the allegiance of the Volunteers as crucial to the success of their respective versions of 'reform'.

Behind the splendour, however, splits remained. Some Belfast merchants had already moved away from the aristocratic Whig leadership and formed their own club, 'The Whigs of Belfast'.[27] The more advanced radicals in the Volunteers went even further and established an alternative organisation. Echoing Drennan's idea of 1785, they formed a 'secret committee' of Belfast Volunteers. These men wanted to transform what they saw as Whig Club electioneering effectively to unite Volunteers and reformers behind a radical programme which included Catholic emancipation. They had asked Wolfe Tone to draft pro-emancipation resolutions to be put to the Bastille day marchers. Although these were rejected by the majority of the Volunteers on 14 July, the secret committee invited Tone back to Belfast in October, a momentous visit which saw the formation of the first United Irish society.[28]

This quickening of political activity also triggered a Volunteering revival. New corps were formed and older ones re-activated. Meetings were called and radical sounding declarations in favour of reform and emancipation were published in the newspapers. Both Belfast Volunteer companies began openly admitting Catholics and the First Company changed their red uniforms for green around August 1791.[29] The Downpatrick Volunteers issued resolutions saying they had 'no hostile intentions against their Roman Catholic fellow-subjects'; that they rejoiced in the prospect of repeal of the penal laws and delighted in the triumph of the French people.[30] The Spa Ballynahinch Volunteers insisted that they were not arming to alarm their Roman Catholic fellow subjects, but rather to protect them.[31]

There were also demonstrations which echoed the 1780s tactic of using public ceremonial for implicit sabre-rattling. Both Belfast Volunteer companies gathered outside the White Linen Hall at noon on 2 November 1792 and rent the gloomy afternoon with three *feux de joie*, to celebrate French army's success against Austria and Prussia. They then met inside and agreed unequivocal revolutionary resolutions: 'We are taxed, tyth'd and enslaved, but we only have to unite and be free'. Later on, as the autumn night drew in, the houses were illuminated by candles placed in windows and, as much in testimony to the ingenuity of the townsfolk as to their politics, by 'transparencies' which shone out in the dark streets bearing slogans such as 'Vive la République', 'Vive la Nation', 'Church and State separated' and, prophetically, 'Union amongst Irishmen'.[32] Following on from this extravaganza a new body was formed in February 1793, calling itself the First Belfast Regiment of the National Guards.[33] Similar 'National' Volunteer corps were formed in Newry, Derry City and Dublin.[34] The term 'National Guard' was a direct imitation of

France's citizen soldiers, hence it directly threatened revolution. Another Volunteer convention was planned for 15 February 1793 at Dungannon – the 11th anniversary of the famous 1782 gathering. This new convention passed resolutions advocating radical reform and complete emancipation, sentiments which appeared to endorse the programme for radical reform produced by the United Irishmen back in October 1791. This begs questions about the relationship between the two organisations. Were they synonymous?

THE VOLUNTEERS AND THE UNITED IRISHMEN

Between the formation of the United Irishmen in 1791 and the start of war with France in 1793, both organisations coexisted as open and legal societies. The former operated as an extra-parliamentary pressure group dedicated to achieving parliamentary reform and emancipation. A strong connection is often assumed, as it is well-known that the impetus behind much of the Volunteer revival in the 1790s came from United Irishmen.[35] However, as so often, the simplicity of retrospective assumptions obscures the more complex contemporary realities. Although the sartorial revolution from red uniforms to green was sudden and conspicuously dramatic, many of those wearing them found themselves marching away from the simplicity and safety of street theatre, mock battles and petitions into unfamiliar territory where the boundaries between constitutional reform and republican revolution were blurred and constantly changing and where the meaning of familiar concepts like 'liberty' and the 'sovereignty of the people' was being manipulated.

Recent research has unravelled some complex strands in the United Irish-Volunteer relationship. Drennan, who influenced the Belfast Volunteers' 'secret committee', wanted a French-backed insurrection long before this became official United Irish policy. Such advanced republicans saw the Volunteers as crucial to success. Lord Edward Fitzgerald and the Sheares brothers went to Paris in November 1792 where, as a self-styled 'Committee of Revolution', they told the Directory that the Volunteers were the agents of revolution in Ireland.[36] They had some basis for this as the *Northern Star* reported that the Belfast Volunteers were trying to buy new arms.[37] However, it is important to realise that the organisations at the polarities of Volunteering – the radical 'secret committee' and the moderate Whig

Clubs – each intended to give a lead to the bulk of the original movement which stood on an unstable centre ground. Many Volunteers,
including some who had joined the United Irish society as a reform
club, while they still wanted political change, resisted being convert-
ed into a French-style revolutionary National Guard.[38] There was
therefore a wide gap between how the advanced United Irishmen saw
the Volunteers and how most Volunteers saw themselves.

The question of how far the revived Volunteers of 1791–93, taken
as a whole, actually differed in nature from the men of 1782 depends
on the angle they are viewed from. In numerical terms, the fact that
delegates from all northern counties could attend a convention, and
the plethora of resolutions appearing in the *Northern Star*, certainly
indicate that, though lacking the massive popular support of 1782,
revived Volunteering nevertheless appealed to significant numbers.
The revived movement's objectives, seen in the 1793 Dungannon resolutions, show that they certainly had moved well away from the
Charlemontite line on the Catholic issue, which opposed full
Catholic relief of the sort proposed by Tone. While accepting that
religious liberty was one of the objects of the Volunteers of 1782, the
moderates retained a residual distrust of Catholics and felt that it
should only be granted piecemeal from 'time to time' and certainly
not at the present time. However, though Charlemont's influence had
severely declined, this does not mean that United Irishmen and radicals dominated the Volunteer agenda in 1793. Although erstwhile
revolutionaries like the Reverend Steel Dickson were present at
Dungannon, so too were some members of the northern landed gentry who kept a wary eye on proceedings.[39]

The turn of events in France clearly had a salutary effect on many
of the Volunteer delegates. The execution of the French king Louis
XVI in January 1793 and the revolutionary government's declaration
of war on Britain and Ireland made many question their vision of the
French Revolution as a new dawn. Significantly the 1793 convention
not only passed a resolution disapproving of the republican system of
government, but bitterly resisted a counter resolution aimed at secur-
ing support for France.[40] Moreover the progress of the 'National
Volunteers' indicated that they were very much a fringe element in
Volunteering. Lord Edward Fitzgerald told the French that a force of
4,000 republican Volunteers could be reckoned on if French support
was forthcoming. Archibald Hamilton Rowan extravagantly hoped

for a membership of 6–10,000 National Volunteers but Drennan more prosaically and more accurately reckoned that they could only muster 200.[41] Even Edward Cooke's informants gave the impression of heady romanticism rather than imminent revolution. An anonymous letter described to the congenitally suspicious Castle undersecretary how Hamilton Rowan had ordered a Dublin tailor, Grace of Cutpurse Row, to make 1,000 hats at five shillings and five pence and the same number of cockades at one shilling and seven pence halfpenny each and that several hundred had been ordered for National Volunteers in the north. Significantly he noted that 200 had been collected, which seems to confirm Drennan's gloomy prediction.[42] This poor showing belied the enthusiasm the Belfast Volunteeers had tried to ignite in November with their display of illuminations and transparencies bearing radical political slogans. The rejection of republicanism and separatism at Dungannon, plus the poor showing of the 'National Volunteers' shows that things were changing fast. Unlike the successfully constructed unanimity of 1782, the leadership of revived Volunteering was being contended for by different groups and the movement lacked overall political direction. Indeed, if any direction was emerging, it was a resurrection of the wartime patriotism which motivated the original Volunteers in 1778.

THE SUPPRESSION OF THE VOLUNTEERS, 1793

Assumptions about the potential of armed citizens in an age of revolution were not confined to the United Irishmen. The government had for some time been watching the revived movement anxiously. Their alarm increased when the bellicose text of a Volunteer address written by Drennan was published.[43] The authorities struck first in Dublin where Volunteering was suppressed by proclamation in January 1793. Their Belfast counterparts suffered the same fate in March. Legislation followed banning delegate conventions, armed associations and the import of arms and gunpowder.[44] Despite warlike noises, particularly from Belfast, the Volunteers actually accepted their suppression quietly, though a military riot in the town in March 1793 was clearly intended to convince the more resolute that the government meant business. This passivity provides still more evidence that most Volunteers were re-evaluating their role now that the brave new world of Belfast Bastille day in 1791 was rapidly becoming a dangerous one.

The fact that Volunteering was at a transitional phase at the point when it was suppressed would have significance in the years preceding the 1798 rebellion. The ban meant the Volunteer story abruptly ended before it had reached its natural conclusion. This untidy end meant that when the allegiance of ex-Volunteers was sought, as it would soon be, by the different 'sides' to the forthcoming conflict, each could present diametrically opposed versions of the real meaning of 'the Volunteers'.

The United Irish movement was itself undergoing profound change at this time. Their reform plan was rejected by parliament in 1794 and the organisation was suppressed the same year when the government obtained definite proof of the long-suspected French connection. The United Irishmen responded by reorganising on military lines as a mass-based underground revolutionary secret society.[45] Because of their previous military experience and access to weapons, ex-Volunteers were soon seen as pearls of great price by the newly-militarised United movement. However, the 'unfinished history' of the Volunteers allowed the United Irishmen to appeal not just to the green-jacketed National Volunteers but to the whole original organisation. These appeals appeared in the columns of the *Northern Star*. In June 1796 the *Star* suggested that the 'birthday' of the United Irishmen was 15 February 1782, the date of the Dungannon Resolutions.[46] The propaganda significance of 1782 was twofold. Not only did it remind Volunteers of their great triumph, redolent of their radical 'True Whig' tradition partly based on John Locke's theory of the citizen's right to resist arbitrary government, but it also recalled that the Dungannon Resolutions 'rejoiced in the relaxation' of the penal laws. Emancipation was amongst the United Irishmen's earliest political demands but when we recall that they were now establishing a military alliance with the Catholic Defenders[47] the true nature of the appeal to the Volunteers becomes clear. Ideology and tradition were being exploited for military ends.

Up to mid-1796 the United Irishmen had one decided advantage in their bid to enlist uncommitted ex-Volunteers: the Irish government, itself remembering 1782, was terrified of all Volunteering. In the years following the French Revolution, the notion of allowing citizens to combine and arm of their own volition was seen as extremely dangerous by the governing classes. Back in 1795 the lord lieutenant, Camden, had stamped out anti-Defender associations on the grounds that they might start what he called 'a new system of Volunteering' which would be outside the government's control.[48] The *Star* was quick to make this official phobia a recruiting sergeant for the Union by playing on Volunteering pride, reminding ex-Volunteers of their suppression in 1793: 'Alas Volunteers you were PUT DOWN'.[49] Yet, with Ireland's regular garrison now profoundly depleted by the demands of the overseas war and with the Irish militia[50] considered unreliable, as the domestic crisis deepened, Camden was forced to consider organising another defence force from the indigenous population.

LORD CHARLEMONT AND HOME DEFENCE, 1796

The government were well aware that the United Irishmen and Defenders were amalgamating for rebellion and that a French invasion was imminent. Camden faced an appalling dilemma. The demands of counter-insurgency, which necessitated troops to be dispersed in small detachments, and anti-invasion contingency plans, which needed a large, gathered army ready to march speedily to the coast, were militarily and strategically antithetical.[51] The Irish government had inadequate manpower to cope with this problem. Regular troops were in short supply because of the war. The Irish militia was felt to be unreliable, and open to infiltration by the United Irishmen and Defenders. It had been raised in 1793 and was, in the southern regiments which served in the north, largely Catholic in the ranks. Fencible regiments, troops raised in Britain for wartime service in the three kingdoms, were considered poor quality soldiers. This meant the government had to look again at locally-raised forces. Apart from the Volunteers, more recent precedents abounded. One of the defining features of the Revolutionary and Napoleonic wars was the huge expansion of the military potential of the participants by the enlistment of civilians – those who would not normally have become soldiers – into their armed forces. France had set the lead with the *Levée en Masse* of 1793 which raised half a million men.[52] An English yeomanry cavalry was raised in the shires in 1794 and Volunteer infantry units were also organised. In Ireland the troop shortages, fears about the militia and the worsening internal security situation had thrown the demise of Volunteering into sharp relief for local

Lord Charlemont

magistrates who faced intimidation of juries, arms raids, attacks on their own persons and, in mid-Ulster, ongoing sectarian feuding.

The Volunteers had provided a police-type force and the need for something similar began to be severely felt. *Ad hoc* law and order associations started in parts of Ulster, but these could only be temporary and uncoordinated as anything systematic would immediately have Camden seeing the ghosts of 1782. The government began cautiously to consider a local defence force modelled on the English yeoman

ASSOCIATION of the INHABITANTS of the Town of DUNGANNON, to Support and Defend the KING and CONSTITUTION, to preserve the Peace of their Town and its Neighbourhood, and to discourage and resist all Endeavours to excite Sedition and Rebellion.

WHEREAS, we have observed with much concern that great pains have been taken of late in many parts of this Country, to excite discontents among his Majesty's faithful subjects, thereby to alienate their affections from his Person and Government, and to induce them to be willing to exchange our excellent free Constitution, for that System of Anarchy and Confusion, which is now spreading desolation over other parts of the world.

AND WHEREAS, we have reason to believe, that some miscreants have carried their wickedness so far as to hold treasonable correspondence with the French, with whom his Majesty is now at open War, to invite them to invade this Kingdom; and, as an encouragement, have held out the following audacious falsehood, viz. that his Majesty's subjects in this Kingdom are ready to rebel against him, and to adopt their principles, and that a few, seduced by the emissaries of the French, through the management of a desperate and traiterous Society, have bound themselves by oaths to be ready, (in furtherance of these purposes) in case of Invasion, either to join them, or to rise and take possession of the Country, and the property of its peaceable Inhabitants.

NOW we whose names are hereunto subscribed, Inhabitants of the Town of Dungannon, sincerely attached to our most excellent Constitution, sensible of the benefits we enjoy under the mild Government of our most Gracious Sovereign, and of the present prosperous state of our Country, prosperous in a degree heretofore unexampled, where Wealth and Comfort are sure to follow honest Industry, unwilling to put at hazard these solid advantages, and abhorrent of the machinations of a set of desperate adventurers, who without Property themselves aim at that of others, and hope to rise to wealth and consequence in a general Confusion.

RESOLVE, that we will at the hazard of our Lives and Fortunes support and defend our Gracious KING GEORGE the Third, against all Foreign and Domestic Enemies.

THAT we will discourage and oppose all treasonable and seditious practices, and resist all attempts to disturb the peace of the Country.

AND further in case of actual Invasion, or Insurrection, should his Majesty in his wisdom require such Exertion, THAT WE WILL EMBODY OURSELVES FOR HIS DEFENCE, AND FOR THE PROTECTION OF OUR TOWN, and all of us, or as many of us as he shall think fit to call upon, will enroll ourselves under such Officers as he shall Commission, and with their assistance, and under their Command will train and discipline ourselves, so as to be able to render him the more effectual service, and frustrate the hopes of the Traitors and Banditti, who vainly rely upon finding the Country naked and defenceless, should the regular Troops be drawn off to oppose an invading Enemy.

HERE follow the names of the associators, too numerous to be inserted.

Session House, Dungannon, July 12, 1796.

WE, the JUSTICES OF THE PEACE for the County of Tyrone, assembled at the Quarter-Sessions, unanimously approve of the above resolutions, and warmly recommend the adoption of them to the different Towns and Parishes of this County.

NORTHLAND	JOHN STAPLES	T. CAULFIELD	JAMES RICHARDSON
CASTLESTEWART	ROBERT LOWRY	EDWARD EVANS	T. K. HANNINGTON
JAMES STEWART	R. LINDSAY	A. STEWART	W. T. ARMSTRONG
T. KNOX	JAMES VERNER	T. FORESYTHE	SAMUEL STREAN

Resolutions of the Dungannon Association

cavalry. The intention was that a similar force in Ireland would be trustworthy, because of its property connections and, crucially, different from the Volunteers, who had been largely infantry. The notion of a property-based force found strong support among Camden's 'cabinet' of advisers, particularly the Speaker, John Foster. However, despite Camden's palpable reticence, events on the ground made it clear that, if an Irish Yeomanry force were to be raised, the key to its success was held by ex-Volunteers.

During August 1796, the government 'felt the pulse' of Protestant opinion with a canvass of the localities to see what support there was for such a force. There was, as would be expected, no shortage of advice and some actual offers of service. One of the most fully-formed of these came from Dungannon, the old Volunteering Mecca, but with the critical difference that this service was to be under officers commissioned by the government and therefore not independent as had been the case in the 1770s.[53] This offer was for infantry service: the canvass had revealed that there were so few wealthy English-type horse-owning 'yeomen' farmers that if the government limited service to them, the plan would fail. Early in September Camden was called on by Charlemont who voiced similar concerns. Shortly afterwards a key decision was taken that infantry as well as cavalry corps were to be allowed in a yeomanry force which, if it were to succeed, would have to be raised substantially on the structures of the old Volunteering movement.[54]

This decision marked a revolution in Camden's thinking: the beginnings of a rapprochement between the Castle and the Volunteers. The government could now engage in the propaganda battle to gather manpower. Charlemont's name was used to 'advertise' the yeomanry force as one which ex-Volunteers could conscientiously join. The chief secretary, Pelham, privately admitted that the use of Charlemont was 'calculated to reconcile those who had been eager promoters of the old Volunteers'.[55] This reconciliation was a change of tactics rather than a change of heart, as the government, having publicly committed itself to raising a yeomanry, risked handing the United Irishmen a moral victory if the plan backfired through insufficient public support. Their use of Charlemont therefore had decidedly political overtones. Charlemont opposed Camden's government politically and detested its coercive policies. He was however no stooge, and insisted that his involvement in the yeomanry did not prejudice his right to criticise what he saw as the misgovernment of Ireland. As he had done in past crises, Charlemont put defence before politics and adopted the attitude that if England's difficulty was revolutionary France's opportunity it could not also be Ireland's. 'Would I refuse to bear a hand in stopping a leak in a sinking vessel' he asked Haliday rhetorically, 'because I hated the commander?'[56]

With Charlemont on board and the cavalry-only stance dropped, the government followed up with other adjustments to capitalise on the inroads already made. Volunteer corps had elected their officers; indeed historians point to this as evidence of their 'democratic' nature. Initially the government prevented these practices in the yeomanry, but it now moved quickly to head off potential opposition by a further compromise which accepted the election of officers. Indeed, some yeomanry corps went so far as formally to embody the practice in their own internal rules. James Stewart of Killymoon's corps 'appointed' Stewart as their commander and declared 'all other officers will be elected by ballot'.[57]

However, the real test of the success of the government's bid for uncommitted ex-Volunteers was whether they could prevent them either from being enlisted by the United Irishmen or imbued with sufficient doubt to stop them joining the yeomanry. Everyone knew this battle would be won or lost in the North. In Armagh, when the yeomanry was being canvassed in September, the United Irishmen tried to discourage Charlemont's old Volunteers by spreading rumours that the yeomanry oath of allegiance was a trap to get people to support coercion.[58] Charlemont's arrival in Armagh city in early November 1796 saw this campaign and its legalistic arguments intensified by the printing and distribution of handbills appealing to the 1782 spirit, addressed 'To the Yeomanry', and 'To the Earl of Charlemont'. However, the government's new stance gave it propaganda ammunition: within hours counter hand-bills appeared on the streets assuring those who signed the oath that this would not prevent them pursuing parliamentary reform by constitutional means.[59] This particular conflict was resolved in favour of the government; yeomanry corps were raised in Armagh reflecting a broad spectrum of political opinion in the city, ranging from Ascendancy Protestants who supported the Primate (and who themselves had been Volunteers) to radical ex-Volunteers who had recently been supporting the French to the extent of planting a liberty tree in the main

EARL OF CHARLEMONT

AS your lordship has again come forward in a public capacity, as patron of the Yeomen Soldiery of this County, I think it my duty to address you on the subject.

Your Lordship having now canvassed the greatest part of the County must be perfectly sensible how the great Body of People stand affected to the measures of the present administration; from the success you have met with, which your Lordship must see is far short of what you expected, and which you once would have experienced, when you enjoyed the confidence of that Band of PATRIOTS the VOLUNTEERS of Ireland, to whom the Nation is indebted for sowing the first seeds of UNION among Irishmen, which cannot now be prevented, ripening into maturity, and which had the Volunteers enjoyed, they could never have been put down by all the arts of a corrupt and profligate administration.

Indeed my Lord, did you know how tired the people of Ireland are of cabals and dissentions under religious pretences, which have been encouraged to promote the interests of those men whose strength is the WEAKNESS and DIVISIONS of the Kingdom and did you know how willing the People are now to assemble under the Olive Branch of Peace and Good will, and that they are Determined that religion shall no longer be a Pretence for a man to live at enmity with his neighbour; and did you know my lord, how far that great National benefit THE UNION OF IRISHMEN has already been accomplished, you would not now attempt to come forward as the dupe of these men from whom you have received such repeated insults, and who must not only have wounded the feelings of your lordship, but also the feelings of every Volunteer whom you had the honour to command.

Surely your lordship cannot so soon have forgot the time you were ignominiously deprived of the honour of being Governor of this county, [an honour which your ancestors had enjoyed for centuries] and a man preferred over your head, of whose ancestors there is little on record, except that they compared the people to mules; and whose self might still have remained in obscurity, was it not for the speech he had the honour of DELIVERING in favour of the persecuted Catholics of this county; and he might have enjoyed his insignificance under the splendour of a coronet, which any Nabob could purchase, though he had acquired the means by the most cruel abuse of power, and at the expence of humanity.

I mean not however to compare your lordships character with the one just mentioned, your title may be traced through an honourable and virtuous ancestry, and till of late has been supported by your lordship, with equal dignity, but we are now sorry to see your lordship forfeit the Confidence and Esteem of that People [who once considered you the Father of the Country] by joining with those men, who have subverted the dearest Rights of the Nation, and heaped insults upon every man who had the Virtue or Honesty to withstand their unjust measures.

Your lordship may be led to think that because the people of this city (when thinking of your former services) have so very generously offered their lives and fortunes at your lordships service, that they ought to follow up their resolutions by becoming Yeomen-Soldiers; but in that, fear, your lordship has been much disappointed; for, although the people may have entertained ever so warm an affection for your lordship, yet when, contrary to every sentiment of honour you will attach yourself to those men who have defaced every beauty of our Constitution, and have brought our liberty to the shadow of a name, you cannot expect that the people will be so very forgiving as your lordship, and wheel about in defence of those men, their pensions, and their sinecures; no, my lord, the people's grievances lie heavier on them, and they feel the force of a Convention bill—a Gun-Powder Bill—an Insurrection Bill—and lastly, the repealing of the Habeas Corpus Act, too well to be duped by that Administration (as your lordship has been who by their unjust measures, reduced the best informed part of the nation to a state bordering on Insurrection, from which they cannot be removed, until the people are restored to their Primitive Rights in the Legislature.

A CITIZEN OF ARMAGH.

United Irish handbill, November 1796

street.[60] Given that Camden originally would not have had a yeomanry that bore any resemblance to the Volunteers, either in uniform, structure or ethos, the fact that reformers were now being actively courted by means of their own Volunteering tradition shows not only how far Camden had moved in a few short months. It also shows how far he needed to move.

This strategic policy shift can also be seen in the resolutions published at meetings held to raise yeomen. Originally the meetings produced standardised resolutions, steering clear of any political comment that strayed from the platitudes about King, Country and Constitution, as typified by the 1796 Dungannon offer of service. At around the same time as the argument was being turned against the United Irishmen in Armagh, in County Down Lord Castlereagh and his father Lord Londonderry were having problems raising yeomanry from their tenantry. The Newtownards area was a heavily Presbyterian district with strong Volunteering traditions, where the corps had continued into the 1790s and become extremely radical and pro-French. The Stewarts had once enjoyed Volunteer support when, in the early 1790s, they took the independent, reforming line in county politics. However, from about 1794 they turned to the government side and relations with their tenants deteriorated, many of whom began supporting the United Irishmen. Initially Castlereagh and Lord Londonderry could get few of the tenantry to take the oath and offer as yeomen, but eventually, after much canvassing, persuaded several hundred of them to take it and selected 53 for a yeomanry corps. However the resolutions these Newtownards yeomen signed were significantly different from those of, for example, the Dungannon Association[61], and read like a reformer's manifesto. Like Charlemont's old Armagh Volunteers, the Newtownards men quibbled over the oath, noting that: 'As we cannot come forward under the present laws as an armed association without first taking the oath of allegiance contained in the act ... we will not hesitate to take that oath ... [but] in doing so we do not consider ourselves as pledged to desist from seeking every constitutional method of obtaining a repeal of many laws we consider as very obnoxious and indeed encroachments on the very spirit and essence of the constitution'.[62] These developments were a setback for the United Irishmen. However, one key place remained to stop the rot: the northern capital of republicanism, the town the Marquess of Downshire once called 'that damned sink of

Belfast'.[63]

THE STRUGGLE FOR A BELFAST YEOMANRY

Given the background of radicalism in the town's Volunteers it was only to be expected that yeomanry would prove difficult to raise in Belfast; nor indeed was it surprising that the struggle happened later here than elsewhere. Belfast was the citadel of northern radicalism, to be held or taken at all costs: it would not be stretching credulity to argue that it held the key to United Irish military success.

When the yeomanry plan was being canvassed in other places, there had been some tentative moves in Belfast, but they were smartly rebuffed. In early September 1796 Castlereagh circulated a petition of loyalty for the townspeople to sign. Some did; but many refused, claiming they were discontented at the government's refusal to grant reform. Charlemont remarked acidly, 'Is it merely a spirit of discontent, I also am discontented', and concluded pessimistically, 'There was a time when my opinion might have had some little weight in Belfast, but, alas, those halcyon days are fled'.[64] Another opportunity came in mid-September, following the arrest of prominent United Irishmen, including the young Charles Teeling, under the emergency powers afforded by the suspension of Habeas Corpus. A town meeting was mooted to protest against this 'indignity to the civil power' and express willingness to preserve the peace and to campaign for reform by solely peaceful means. Martha McTier saw the hand of Charlemont at work. She was William Drennan's sister, married to the United Irishman, Samuel McTier, and was an intelligent, well-informed, if somewhat ascerbic commentator on Belfast affairs. Martha told her brother how 'two moderate gentlemen' had handed about the requisition for the meeting and showed two pre-prepared resolutions, 'the first purporting surprise, and some little degree of resentment [at the arrests] … asserting it [Belfast] to be a place where the laws nor the civil magistrates were never opposed; the second, "that they would arm themselves to protect the peace from (I am not quite sure what) provided they obtained a radical reform"'. She then described how Dr Haliday had signed the requisition and the resolutions were given immediately to his friend and fellow moderate reformer, the Reverend William Bruce, minister of First Belfast Presbyterian Church. Attached to the resolutions was 'a long list of

Reverend William Bruce

names of both parties', some of whom had signed in the belief that by doing so they were supporting the 'stand or fall' resolutions, as Castlereagh's earlier loyal petition was known.[65]

The plan was to draw uncommitted Belfast Volunteers back into the ambit of constitutional politics. The resolutions were intended to give expression to their frustration being full of 'sound and fury' but, like Macbeth's poor player, if not 'signifying nothing' then certainly capable of a different construction than the more radical would have wanted. In short they would have laid the foundation for an offer of yeomanry service. One eye witness told McTier that Bruce had 'the second time made a schism in the politics of Belfast' and, in 'saying every word of the resolutions spoke daggers – though the word radical was left out.' Bruce succeeded in winning the support of John Holmes, Henry Joy, Waddell Cunningham and others. However the plan failed as, in the event, the meeting was aborted, having been deemed dangerous in the already tense situation. Consequently, as Haliday informed Charlemont, 'nothing can be done in the way your Lordship thought eligible'.[66]

Clearly then, given that it came shortly before Charlemont's excursion to angle for the Armagh Volunteers, this ploy to outflank the Belfast extremists was part of a wider process whereby the old commander tried to reclaim his erstwhile followers from those who would make them the foot soldiers of insurrection. Charlemont intended stealing a march on the United Irishmen by using the meeting to propagate the new doctrine that becoming a yeoman did not necessarily mean supporting coercion, nor preclude demanding change by constitutional means. Indeed Charlemont consistently opposed coercion. He became involved with the yeomanry for the same patriotic reasons as had impelled him into the Volunteers: he felt the country was in danger.[67]

Charlemont's supporters were not the only ones supporting the raising of yeomanry in Belfast. On 10 October a petition from the 'distressed loyalists' of Belfast was sent, not to Charlemont, but to Downshire, who had been canvassing for yeomanry in County Down. Although this semi-literate document ended up at Dublin Castle, it cannot be interpreted as mere favour-seeking by the victims of the current war-induced economic crisis.[68] These men were much further down the social scale than either Bruce's supporters or the more radical townsmen, who both came from Belfast's entrepreneurial merchant and textile manufacturing class. The 'distressed loyalists' were probably those who had signed the 'stand or fall' resolutions in September; now, for their trouble, they themselves were in danger of falling into unemployment and destitution. These men were mostly weavers and tradesmen, who complained that the manufacturers were operating a policy of economic intimidation 'because we would not joyn [sic] the Rebels of this town', that 'the work is interely [sic] taken from some of us and the rest expects no more than what is in the loom'.[69] The petition was signed by 64 people offering to become yeomen and included a further 47 named supporters. Downshire's submission of the petition to the Castle shows that he saw it as a potential offer of yeomanry service, similar to many others that were landing on the Chief Secretary's desk at this time. However, nothing came of this either and the prospect for a Belfast yeomanry lay in an agonised stasis, shuddering between the United Irishmen's pikes, Bruce's daggers and the debtor's goal. When the first yeomanry commissions issued from Dublin Castle in October 1796 none were destined for Belfast, where the tense stalemate about yeomanry continued until Christmas when some decidedly less than festive guests made their appearance at Bantry Bay off the south coast of Ireland.

STREET POLITICS: THE BELFAST YEOMANRY MEETINGS

The presence of Wolfe Tone and a large French force riding at anchor off Bantry waiting only for the gales to abate to launch an invasion made home defence a priority throughout Ireland, and a final showdown in Belfast inevitable, regardless of the consequences. On 30 December 1796 the outgoing town sovereign (mayor), John Brown, having received a letter from Dublin Castle saying the French were at Bantry, proposed the formation of yeomanry to the Belfast merchants and businessmen at a meeting held in the Exchange. This meeting was to prove more successful than the previous attempts. To understand why, we need to try to see it in its contemporary setting.

Recent historical research on English urban public assemblies makes the point that they are complex phenomena which cannot be properly understood unless the full background context of the 'crowd event' is established, both in local terms and against the backdrop of national events.[70] The same problems and the same approach have obvious relevance for the Belfast yeomanry meetings of late 1796. The immediate background was obviously the threat of invasion. This was important, not only for the military threat, but also for the political space it gave to allow the supporters of yeomanry to circumvent arguments which had previously branded their motivation as simply collusive coercion. The cry 'government in danger' would not have found many sympathetic ears in Belfast, but 'Ireland in danger' would resonate patriotically and recall the response to previous invasion threats in 1760 and 1778. Indeed it would have echoed those Volunteers at Dungannon in 1793 whose support for France

The Old Exchange, Belfast

ceased at the onset of war. This background also included the whole saga of previous attempts to raise yeomanry and the litany of argument and counter-argument about the yeomanry oath. Finally there was the deepening domestic crisis: Belfast lay under the shadow of the Insurrection Act.[71] Since November the government had been considering, and in some places actually implementing, this draconian Act, which made districts liable to military coercion.[72] Charlemont's conscientious scruples about coercion were not shared by the majority of the 'Ascendancy'; indeed Lord Carhampton, the commander-in-chief, had actually been using the threat of this awesome measure to encourage the formation of yeomanry corps in places like Newry where there was reluctance.[73] General Lake, who believed that Belfast and disaffection were synonymous, also threatened to use the Act to wreck the town, and none of the townspeople doubted that he was both willing and entirely capable of doing precisely that. Rumours were rife in Belfast that the town was to be burned.[74]

The responses to this crisis varied according to the individual. Where Lake relished the excuse to reduce the town to cinders, Charlemont hoped the phoenix patriotism would arise from its ashes. On the other hand, Edward Cooke, who was well informed about

25

Belfast, despaired, saying: 'I would *bribe* almost those who are well disposed in the town to be yeomen'.[75] Viewed against this backdrop, the issue was understandably difficult for the Belfast merchants. They now had finally to decide on the question of whether or not they should form yeomanry corps in the town. Many things had to be balanced. On the one hand were abstract ideological arguments about patriotism; on the other was the issue of survival, both financial and personal. However, looked at pragmatically, both contingencies – the French army's invasion and the Irish government's Insurrection Act – meant pretty much the same thing in terms of their livelihoods. As well as the immediate background, the context of a public assembly also includes the circumstantial detail of the actual meeting or crowd event itself: the time, place, attendance, resolutions and so on. The finer details of the Belfast meeting are well worth analysing. Not only was it charged with high drama and explosive passions, it also provides a wonderful example of late eighteenth-century street politics and crowd manipulation. Most of all, perhaps, it allows a peep behind all the stultifying myths such historical events have accumulated over the last two hundred years. A dispassionate examination of this crucial meeting and its aftermath reveals some answers to Charles Teeling's 'double traitors' accusation.

The most detailed accounts are left by Henry Joy and the antiquarian Samuel McSkimin, who was himself a yeoman.[76] These can be supplemented at various points by the surviving contemporary manuscript and printed evidence. McSkimin tells how John Brown's yeomanry proposal on 30 December 1796 provoked the now well-rehearsed cry about the yeomanry oath. Brown then proposed a public meeting for the following day at the Exchange and handbills were circulated. In consequence, on the last dark day of the ominous year of 1796, 'the great room of the Exchange was crowded to excess'. Brown took the chair to urge yeomanry formation and was supported and followed by the incoming sovereign, the Reverend William Bristow. Bristow reasoned that 'armed associations ... had been generally misunderstood', obviously trying to spin the government-Charlemontite line that yeomanry membership did not preclude campaigning for reform.[77] One can readily imagine the atmosphere as these politically loaded arguments were rehearsed, when, suddenly, a dramatic intervention came from the floor.

William Sampson, a United Irish lawyer, stood up and proposed that a committee should be formed to consider the question. In what was clearly a pre-planned tactic, another United Irishman, Lord Edward Fitzgerald's friend Arthur O'Connor, rose and heatedly supported Sampson. O'Connor denied that the French were at Bantry and proposed that the meeting adjourn to allow the townspeople time to decide. This procedural move was obviously intended to allow the initiative to be seized from government supporters and for the United Irishmen to exert their own pressure. It also bought time: given the utter inadequacy of Ireland's defences, the presence of a large French army on Irish soil arguably might help make up minds in Belfast. The meeting was tumultuous to say the least. Some of the audience objected to O'Connor's intervention on the grounds that he was not a Belfast man.[78] Others reportedly threatened to throw Chichester Skeffington, who supported the raising of yeomanry, from one of the Exchange windows. Some of Skeffington's backers tried to counter-attack and outflank the adjournment device. John Turnley assured the volatile audience that, despite O'Connor's denials, the French were indeed at Bantry. Belfast's post master Thomas Whinnery backed him and proposed opening a book there and then for those who were pre-pared to become yeomen. The committee that resulted from the first meeting was as odd as a pantomime horse, including in its ungainly bulk Brown and Bristow along with known United men such as William Tennant, Gilbert McIlveen, Robert Simms and Sampson and O'Connor. However, this incredible creature was no figure of fun, rather it was intended as a cover for deadly serious United Irish mili-tary strategy.

When the meeting reconvened on 2 January 1797, Sampson's plan was working and Bristow and Brown, their position made impossible from the onset, had withdrawn from the committee. In the interven-ing period between the meetings, the short days and long nights of whispered rumour, insinuated threat, influence and intrigue meant that the crowd which gathered was so large that the Exchange could not accommodate them and the meeting had to be shifted to the White Linen Hall. McSkimin implies this shift of location was acci-dental, saying there were no arrangements at the Linen Hall to receive 'such a multitude' and the crowd consequently assembled on the street outside.[79] However, a strong element of deliberate engineering can be detected when it is considered how much it was in the inter-ests of those against raising yeomanry to make a large and public display of opposition; whereas the cause of those trying to nurture it to life was best served by remaining behind closed doors till the birth was over. Martha McTier's account of the affair vividly conveys the impression of crowd choreography. She said the Linen Hall was refused them and so 'the matter was settled in the street'. With Bristow not to be found, a chair was procured, Sampson put on it and 'the resolutions prepared passed'.[80]

As Volunteer parades demonstrated, politicised crowd activity was a feature of the later eighteenth century. Crowd manipulation had recently become an essential part of the United Irish propaganda armoury with the famous 'potato diggings'.[81] Moreover the first July Orange demonstrations in 1796 showed that the occupation of public space itself was now imbued with political significance. The White Linen Hall had traditionally been the focal point of parades, indeed the street outside it, where Sampson's crowd gathered, was holy ground for the Belfast Volunteers. This piece of street theatre was no spontaneous performance; it had been well-rehearsed and, with public opinion whipped up, the non-attendance of Bristow had been already written into the script.

The government supporters having withdrawn, the stage was open to Sampson who, obviously relishing his role, regaled the crowd outside the Linen Hall. Drennan remarked, not altogether approvingly, on his populist tactics, noting wryly: 'If I be the quietest man in Ireland, [an allusion to his seditious libel trial] Sampson is certainly the most active, that can leap upon a joint stool and harangue the population'.[82] This implication of rabble-rousing ties in with Chichester Skeffington's report of the first meeting in which he claims that Sampson railroaded the meeting by arranging for what he called 'an influx of the lower classes'.[83] The subsequent crowd outside the Linen Hall also seems to have contained a wide social mixture and Sampson was not beneath exploiting the inherent social tensions as the means towards his end of preventing yeomanry being raised in Belfast. Both Joy's and McSkimin's accounts agree that Sampson pointedly remarked on the presence of 'so many wealthy and distinguished men' in the Linen Hall crowd. However, it soon became clear that Sampson was setting them up as a means to manipluate the bulk of the crowd, as he then expressed regret that there were not even more poor people present, implying that their genuine patriotism would stand in contrast to those 'who affect to look down upon you and despise you'.[84] Having insinuated aristocracy, usually a trump card in Presbyterian Belfast, Sampson went on to ask if they would follow Charlemont's example and 'offer their lives to government without any qualification'. He then reminded them 'that it was not Lord Charlemont that raised the Volunteers, it was the Volunteers that raised Lord Charlemont' and, nearer to home, recalled Lake's threat 'to have your town demolished … unless you forced your consciences to take the oath.'[85]

Sampson was simultaneously trying to harness economic discontent to make a class-based argument against yeomanry and attempting to attract the old Belfast Volunteers by reverting to the ideological argument about what the genuine Volunteer spirit meant. Leaving aside the stunning irony that wealthy United Irish textile manufacturers had recently been exploiting their control of capital to prevent weavers from joining the yeomanry, the inconsistency in Sampson's appeal to the lower classes was of course that the original Belfast Volunteers had been men with sufficient property to feel the need to defend it. However, in the heat of the moment, most people would not have had time to reflect on such matters. Sampson had generated sufficient impetus and emotional energy in the street to get the job done before Lake had time to react. After his 'harangue', Sampson was called to the chair and six pre-prepared resolutions were rapidly read and passed. These basically blamed the state of the country on the unreformed parliament and offered to 'arm in like manner as the Volunteers, whose memory we revere, and whose example we wish to imitate'.[86] Sampson's legalistic mind was working overtime: to add a final exquisite twist and thereby wring out the maximum propaganda value, the proper legal procedures were to be followed. Sampson, as chairman, was requested to take the resolutions to John Brown for transmission to the lord lieutenant. However this was one offer Brown could not accept and he refused to be the bearer of such disingenuous propaganda.[87] Notwithstanding Brown's refusal, the resolutions were published on 5 January in the *Northern Star* and the *Dublin Evening Post*.[88] Sampson's triumph, however, turned out to be something of a Pyrrhic victory.

Meanwhile a much smaller number had signed counter-resolutions, composed by Chichester Skeffington, to form a yeomanry corps. Perhaps if the French had landed, Sampson's propaganda coup would have been turned into a military victory; however, in the long road to rebellion, even if the numbers were few, a precedent was set and the pattern of refusal was broken. The numbers were indeed small. Although McSkimin says the book Whinnery opened at the Exchange meeting had 120 signatures, it seems hindsight had distorted his memory.[89] According to official reports, Skeffington's petition lay at the Exchange Coffee House for two days, by which time it had only collected 53 signatures, a number which took until 12 January 1797 to become 100 and only reached 150 later in the month.[90] This figure was not exactly impressive, considering Edward Cooke's recent calculations about Belfast's manpower potential. Cooke reckoned that of Belfast's population of 18,000 there were 4,500 men of fighting age, of which 1,600 were already sworn United Irishmen.[91] Moreover, Skeffington's men used every bit as much emotional and psychological pressure as their opponents. Colonel Barber admitted that 'much intrigue and interest' had been exerted.[92] Yet from this small and somewhat tardy group, a cavalry and an infantry corps were formed and the nucleus of a local defence force established which was to grow as the count-down to rebellion began in earnest.

'DOUBLE TRAITORS' OR REAL VOLUNTEERS?

What does the Belfast yeomanry meeting tell us? Were these men indeed the archetypes of Teeling's 'double traitors' or were they true to Volunteering principles? These are crucial questions, given the military importance of the old Volunteers and the strategic and symbolic significance of Belfast. The copious contemporary commentary the Belfast yeomanry meeting generated reveals just how central was the issue of what Volunteering *meant* in the war of words that preceded the war with pikes and muskets in 1798.

As we have seen, the United Irishmen had long claimed to be heirs to the genuine Volunteer tradition, the 'spirit' of 1782. However, this appropriation became a bone of contention after Charlemont's decision to back the yeomanry in September 1796. Proprietorial claims to the *authentic* Volunteer tradition soon came from every side. The government paper, the *Freeman's Journal*, lauded the fact that yeomanry were being raised by Charlemont, 'general of the *original* Volunteers'. Attempting to draw a line between 'the Volunteers of Ireland' and later 'spurious crew of accoutered ragamuffins', the *Freeman* asserted that 'those desperadoes were indeed disarmed and the real Volunteers should feel themselves honoured on the degradation'.[93] Sampson, from the opposite political perspective, had approvingly noted the presence of the 'genuine originators of the Volunteers' in the crowd at the Linen Hall.[94]

Following the Belfast meetings, the true meaning of Volunteering was haggled over in pamphlets and letters to newspapers. In early January 1797, a Castle insider, signing himself 'An Irishman', high-lighted the fact that the French were at Bantry while the meeting was going on, and appealed to Volunteering patriotism, asking if those who got the names of the Belfast men on the resolutions did 'justice to your *real* principles ... are they [Sampson's supporters] to be entrusted with arms upon terms which were not even expected by the [Dublin] Lawyers' corps?' This provoked a riposte by 'A Townsman', which began by evoking civic pride at the effrontery of a Dubliner 'unacquainted with the good sense which characterises Belfast.' The anonymous author claimed that 'perhaps this very Yeoman Act and the coercion used to procure Volunteers under it may have encour-aged them [the French]', then noted significantly that 'the first prin-ciple of the old Volunteers was not to take any military oath, or to be the soldiers of government; or to receive their pay'. The writer, him-self an ex-Volunteer, continued, 'Let anyone who was witness to the spirit of calling forth the original Irish Volunteers – those of this town now the object of such calumny – let him compare it with the means by which these new levies are raised'.[95] Charlemont himself entered the fray, giving his own definition of the Volunteer as a man for all seasons: 'who, unusurped by interest or ambition, acts unbiasedly in his best opinion as to the best way of serving his country ... ever suit-ing his conduct to the exigency of the times ... he is the true patriot'.[96] The debate over whether genuine Volunteers could conscientiously take the yeomanry oath raged on for weeks between 'Veritas' in the *Northern Star* and 'An Old Whig' in the *News Letter*.[97]

While all this rhetoric was going on, hard choices were being faced. Some who found the decision was not clear cut were confronted by an appalling moral dilemma. Martha McTier, to her great credit, recognised the predicament. She admitted to Drennan that: 'These are trying times indeed, and the right path becomes complex ... it is all *half* work here, just enough to damn either side ... about a hundred have agreed to arm, many of them old Vo[lunteer]s'. She humanely acknowledged the agony facing 'the brave and honourable

31

man who must either decline arming against a foreign foe or swear to support the present government'. Some saw compromise as the safest course. Bruce adopted an interim position, engaging to join the yeomanry but only actually serve in the event of invasion or insurrection.[98] Others more openly put their mouth where their money was.

Camden received information about the effect of Sampson's 'harangue' and was 'glad to find that … the conduct of the violent have so disgusted and divided those who formerly at least gave them countenance, and that a party is likely to come forward in support of government'.[99] Sampson's rousing mob oratory at the Linen Hall, whatever message it was intended to convey on the street, clearly sent very different signals to many old Volunteers. Their unease reflects the reality that social revolution, the logical endgame of the United Irishmen's hybrid alliance with France and the Defenders, was equally dreaded by many Belfast merchants as by Ascendancy landlords. These men clearly saw that domestic insurrection or French invasion were equally inimical to their business interests, particularly with the example of the Parisian 'terror' before them, where having guillotined the aristocrats, the revolutionaries turned on each other. Martha McTier observed 'I scarcely know what is called a gentleman who is not enrolled … the old moneyed men are subscribing'.[100] This remark chillingly anticipates Henry Joy McCracken's caustic valedictory comment that 'the rich always betray the poor'. Yet it had substance.

When the first Belfast yeomanry commissions were issued on 21 January 1797, an ex-Volunteer, Charles Rankin, was elected captain of the cavalry corps with William Rainey as first lieutenant and Cortlandt Skinner, soon to be General Nugent's father-in-law, as second lieutenant.[101] Rankin was a wealthy Belfast banker who had been in the forefront of the town's radicalism, having chaired meetings in December 1792 which produced the United Irishmen's address to the Volunteers.[102] Downshire had grave doubts about Rankin and tried to get him removed.[103] General Lake was also suspicious noting that Rankin's appointment was 'curious … for a corps of yeomanry'.[104] Yet Rankin himself wrote to Pelham, with all the extravagant zeal of the pragmatic convert, offering not just his services, but also money and his carriage horses to Lake, claiming that in times like this people 'should suspend all political speculations and unite every man in driving from our shores the enemies of social order'.[105] Since he was a businessman, this comment has the ring of truth, as has the

Waddell Cunningham

involvement of another ex-Volunteer and erstwhile radical reformer, the wealthy entrepreneur Waddell Cunningham, who on 4 April was commissioned captain of the 4th Belfast Infantry. Membership of the three other infantry corps also reflected Belfast's merchant and business community. The first was captained by Robert Wallace, with Henry Joy McCracken's cousin George Joy as first lieutenant and John Turnley second, while the second and third were captained by John Brown and Narcissus Batt respectively.[106] This property-defence element in the Belfast yeomanry did not escape the attentions of their opponents. The United Irishmen, who had previously evoked Volunteer unity using memories of 1782 to make the Volunteers 'United', now rounded on the turncoats, branding them 'another brand of the footstools of tyranny: the remains of the Old Rotten Aristocratic Volunteers'.[107] By February, the *Northern Star* was printing handbills demonising the yeomen as 'Mamelukes' (an eastern caste of military slave) as a jibe about the loss of their Volunteering independence (see frontispiece).[108] However, such interpretations were only sustainable if a selective, indeed mythic version of Volunteering history was used.

At the centre of this myth was the notion that Protestants and Catholics united for the independence of their country in 1782, an impression, as we have seen, manufactured by Patriot politicians to serve their own agenda. The United Irishmen had strategic reasons to interpret 1782 this way as they endeavoured to cement a military coalition with the Defenders. The United Irishmen were not the only ones to 'remember 1782'. At different points in the first half of the nineteenth century, various versions of the Volunteer myth were produced. As the Catholic emancipation campaign gathered momentum, the memory of the Volunteers was again conjured up. In 1818 John Lawless, one of Daniel O'Connell's 'lieutenants' and editor of the *Belfast Monthly Magazine*, republished Henry Joy and William Bruce's 1794 compilation *Belfast politics* as *Belfast politics enlarged*. The 'enlargement' consisted of an introductory essay addressed to the citizens of Belfast, in which Lawless cites the Belfast Volunteers' reply to their Catholic fellow countrymen which began: 'Let our enmities rest with the bones of our ancestors … let us unite to vindicate the rights of our common nature'.[109] Lawless's motive in using the Volunteers was to try to marshal liberal Protestant support behind the emancipation campaign. This treatment is similar to his leader's own lionising of the Volunteers of 1782; indeed O'Connell's most recent biographer cites this as the major reason for his joining the Dublin Lawyer's Yeoman Infantry in 1797.[110] There is an irony in Lawless's mythic treatment of the Volunteers in his revision of Joy and Bruce, in that Joy himself intended to write a Volunteer history which, had it been published, would have been a moderate reformer's version of the Volunteer myth which would have argued that the revived corps of the 1790s were not really Volunteers at all.[111]

Lawless turned a Nelson's eye to the divisions in Volunteering; he saw no treachery, single or double. The contrast between his treatment of Volunteering and Teeling's exactly ten years later could not be more marked. The reasons may be speculated upon. For one thing, Teeling wrote just before the emancipation bill was passed. Though there was some liberal Protestant support for it, violent resistance was feared at a popular level, particularly from the yeomanry, by that time concentrated almost entirely in the north and heavily Orange in composition. Indeed, this resistance was symbolised by an incident in the summer of 1828, involving Lawless himself. With O'Connell's sanction, he had attempted to expand the Catholic Association into south Ulster by means of an 'invasion' at the head of crowds of Catholic peasantry, but withdrew when it was learned that crowds of armed Orangemen were gathered to confront him at Ballybay, County Monaghan.[112] With emancipation gained in 1829, O'Connell, now campaigning for the repeal of the union, actually started an organisation called the Repeal Volunteers. By this stage, the politically re-activated memory of Volunteering had become bizarrely selective regarding honorary membership. In the early 1840s those joining the Repeal Volunteers received a certificate headed: 'The Volunteers of 1782 Revived'. This included an illustrated hagiography of Volunteer icons which not only resolved the differences between Grattan and Flood (whose disagreements over Volunteering had almost led to a duel), but placed them both in the illustrious company of Owen Roe O'Neill, Patrick Sarsfield and Brian Boru.[113]

Teeling's remarks therefore have to be seen in the context of Catholic emancipation; however, his 'double traitors' accusation remains relevant. Leaving aside such absurd manifestations of the Volunteer myth, Teeling obliges us to look behind the myths and rhetoric and consider Volunteering in its contemporary context. Did those Belfastmen who agreed to provide voluntary military service as Belfast yeomen in 1797 break with their Volunteering past, or does their decision reflect more continuity than change? Were they really so different from the previous generation who provided similar service as Volunteers? Did they sacrifice their political independence on the altar of Castle pay and Castle coercion?

If voluntary military service is conceptualised in a pattern where continuities may be maintained, broken or adapted, perhaps we have a new way to understand the situation in Belfast. Such an interpretation has the decided advantage of allowing us to take a step back from the emotionally charged nomenclature of Volunteer and yeoman and the never-to-be-forgotten, slogan-soliciting years of 1782, 1793 and 1798. The potential in this approach is evident when we compare some similarities between the new yeomanry and the old Volunteers. For one thing, there is strong evidence that there was much more political diversity within the Volunteers than has yet been realised. We can get a clue to the extent of this diversity from the names the various corps gave themselves. These fascinating titles read like a cross section of late eighteenth-century Irish political thought and include Reform battalions, Milesian (i.e. ancient and pure Irish) Volunteers, True Blues, Old Orange Volunteers and Boyne Societies.[114] Even in some of the revived Volunteer corps of the 1790s there was wide diversity. Lord Abercorn heard of one Tyrone corps where, on being asked why they joined, the men gave answers which ranged from asserting the Rights of Man to re-asserting the penal laws.[115] The Belfast yeomanry contained all spectrums of political opinion. Orangeism spread in some corps. James Joy resigned his yeomanry commission because some of his yeomen began to sport Orange ribbons in their tunics and 'damned him if he had any croppy (loyalist slang for a United Irishman) blood in his veins' when ordered to remove them.[116] The Belfast yeomanry also included moderate reformers like Bruce and others, either more radical or less resolute who were reportedly considering taking the United Irish oath in March 1797, as the United movement showed signs of regaining its once dominant position in Belfast.[117]

In their motivation the Belfast yeomen also bore many similarities to their Volunteering predecessors. Although in any voluntary military force of civilians there is necessarily a political dimension, it is mistaken, and itself a product of the Volunteer myth, to see the Volunteers solely in political terms. The military and political aspects co-existed and the prominence each aspect had at any particular point in time during the period 1778–93 fluctuated according to the immediate contemporary context. The background for the first Volunteer corps in 1778 was the troop shortages of the American war and the perceived threat of invasion. In Belfast, the venerable veterans of a previous mobilisation, who had manned Carrickfergus Castle during the Jacobite threat in 1745, supported the recently formed Volunteer corps as evidence of the town's renewed spirit of 'self-defence'.[118] Although the first Belfast corps, and several others, deliberately asserted their independence of government in 1778, the growth of Volunteering in 1779 was determined, not by political considerations, but by the realization that the government were not going to raise a militia. The numerical spread of Volunteering, its endorsement by the 'respectable' landowners and its success as a law and order force all engendered confidence. Once the Volunteers were happy with their ability to secure the country, the context changed and their Patriot leaders were free to re-direct the original self-defence impulse into their own political campaign. The original motivation was not extinct though and remained latent during the 'political' phase of Volunteering. During an invasion scare in 1781, Dublin Castle was inundated with offers of military service from Volunteer companies, with the Belfast Volunteers well to the fore.[119] A revival of wartime patriotism was also evident in 1793 in the refusal of the majority of the Dungannon delegates to back pro-French resolutions. Indeed, given that the threat of invasion was very real in late December 1796 and the likelihood of a concurrent insurrection beyond doubt, the choices facing those Volunteers at Dungannon in 1793 were not dissimilar to the options debated in Belfast's Exchange Rooms. Arguably those joining the Belfast yeomanry were not in any sense reneging on their Volunteer background; rather they were continuing the same sort of wartime patriotism that was an essential part of that background.

Even politically the discontinuities between the Volunteers and the yeomanry can be overstated by putting all the emphasis on 1782 and the attainment of 'legislative independence'. When we shift the focus from the centre to the locality matters do not appear quite so clear cut. Morgan Jellett, a member of the Belfast yeoman cavalry who served during the 1798 rebellion, left a record of his experiences in the corps which provides an insight into its ethos. If one were to substitute names and dates, Jellett could well have been describing the first Belfast Volunteers when he recalled with 'much pride ... the independent and honourable principles of that corps, they appointed their own officers, they admitted no person as a member who had ever belonged to any political party, they performed their duty as soldiers, but did not act the part of partisans.'[120] It is true that Dublin Castle had no sanction over the original Volunteers because they did not owe their existence to government-issued commissions, took no government pay and armed themselves. However, although yeomanry service depended on commissions, it was not true that the balance of power had completely gone from the locality to the centre. Yeomanry service was in effect a negotiation between the central government and the localities and there were still many ways that the yeomen could demonstrate considerable independence. For one thing, the yeoman, unless on permanent duty during emergencies, was not under the Mutiny Act and could resign whenever he wished. Some yeomanry corps, including Jellett's, voluntarily served without pay as the Volunteers had done.[121] Indeed Jellett could equally have been describing any one of a variety of middle-class voluntary organisations from growing towns in Britain and western Europe.

TOWARDS AN ALTERNATIVE INTERPRETATION

Until recently historians have tended to view events in Ireland in isolation and shun comparative studies. Yet, if we accept the continuity thesis, fertile comparisons can be drawn between the emergence of both Volunteers and yeomanry and similar amateur military organisations elsewhere. The Patriots in the Irish parliament had their counterparts in other European countries, including Poland, Belgium and the Netherlands. Indeed in the latter country, they developed an armed civilian militia known as the Free Corps, who adopted the Patriot's political programme demanding democratic reform from the Stadholder.[122] These Free Corps engaged in military display for political purposes and even had a Dungannon-like delegate convention which produced political resolutions, the 'Acts of Association'. Although at a national level, the Dutch Free Corps completely differed from most Irish Volunteers in that they overthrew aristocratic government and, with French aid, established the Batavian republic in 1795, at a local level they were similar. Although the Free Corps claimed to represent 'the people', they were quintessentially middle-class in composition, their officers were town 'burghers' and their rank and file were tradesmen, small merchants and brokers. One prominent historian has described them as 'politically aggressive, but socially conservative weapons', whose real function was 'enforcing the *limits* of popular sovereignty' and 'protecting the property of its mandatories'.[123]

Though on the opposite side of the conflict from the Free Corps the English Volunteer movement of 1793–1815 shared the same urban, middle-class social base and same strong sense of civic pride. In the past, British historians have tended to see the 'national defence patriotism' engendered during the French war as a device adopted by the ruling class to dissipate the challenge from urban radicals. Recent research by John Cookson has found that wartime patriotic activity was originated and controlled, not by the county aristocracy, but by the urban middle classes. Cookson links this to a developing middle-class identity in towns, seen in the growth of a civic-mindedness manifested through Volunteer corps, voluntary societies and public displays marking military or naval victories and royal birthdays. Through such voluntary societies, the middle class 'asserted its influence within an aristocratic regime, moulded an identity out of its own diverse character and preserved its power and authority in the towns against a subordinate population.'[124] Cookson sees amateur military organisations as being the 'pre-eminent town-making force' in a period when 'the status concerns of the middle class and problems of urban growth and order gave town-making greater importance and urgency than ever before.'[125] Belfast was a growing town in the late eighteenth and early nineteenth century, whose mercantile class were indeed concerned with their status and that of their town. Can Belfast's yeomen can be seen in the context of a growing town and the concerns of its mercantile and manufacturing middle classes?

In some ways this configuration fits. One recalls Haliday's comment that the formation of yeomanry corps in Belfast 'evinced the unjust and wicked folly of those who condemned and excommunicated its inhabitants in a mass.'[126] Moreover, the printed resolutions of the Belfast Yeoman Cavalry in 1808, agreed in the very Exchange Rooms which had witnessed the stormy meetings of 1796, simply ooze a self-conscious respectability. This was a club worth joining. Membership could only be solicited if an existing member resigned or died. If a vacancy occurred the aspiring member had to be proposed, seconded and balloted for by a meeting of at least 21 members. If he made it through this selection, the new recruit would doubtless have considered the expense of having to provide himself with clothing and equipment was a small entrance fee to join this urban elite. Though the government normally paid for yeomanry equipment, these men voluntarily agreed to forego this and buy their own equipment which consisted of a sword and belt, pouch and belt, coat case and cloak, military gloves, a horse's nose-bag, haversack, canteen and a military collar.[127] Morgan Jellett recognised the communal and social cachet of being a yeoman, describing his corps as 'the most respectable part of the community that I shall ever be proud of having been honoured by admission as a member'.[128] This sense of social pride and a developing civic culture and consciousness can be seen in many of the activities of the Belfast yeomanry in the early nineteenth century. In 1803 when it was envisaged that the Irish yeomanry should take on a more military role, Belfast's corps threw themselves into marching and drilling. The Belfast Merchants' Infantry appointed an acting adjutant, a Mr Crossley to organise the drills for the town's yeomanry battalion. Accordingly Crossley had some 'brief directions' about drills and manoeuvres printed (they ran to 47 pages) and distributed.[129] Sergeant majors were not a normal feature in the yeomanry, but Narcissus Batt ensured that one was hired and provided with pay whether the yeomanry were on government duty or not with the telling proviso, redolent of self-improvement, that, 'as long as he does it well [drilling the men] he may depend on my best endeavours that his situation at all times will be [good]'.[130] In August 1804 Belfast's yeomanry were reviewed by the then lord lieutenant, Lord Hardwicke. Thomas Robinson, who had painted the Battle of Ballynahinch, depicted this colourful occasion on a huge canvas, now owned by the Belfast Harbour Commissioners. The civic pride generated on such an occasion is graphically conveyed in Robinson's painting which shows the Belfast yeomen drawn up and firing a *feu de joie* to greet Hardwicke.

Underlying all this extravagance was the inevitable voluntary effort. The colours for the various corps were provided for by subscription amongst the members. The taste for public ceremonial grew as time went on. In 1805 officers of the Belfast yeomanry battalion engaged to provide an annual subscription (which raised £101 in its first month) to buy instruments for a yeomanry band and to 'pay all additional expenses attending the corps'.[131] Arguably then, this sort of voluntary activity indicates a broad similarity in the Belfast yeomanry to the tendency observable in contemporary urban amateur military corps elsewhere to become agents of a developing middle-class consciousness allied to a rising civic awareness in a growing town. It would be wrong to press the comparison too hard or too widely. For one thing, many rural yeomanry corps, particularly infantry, bear more resemblance to a feudal levy of a landlord's tenants rather than a proto-democratic voluntary organisation. Moreover, in Belfast, the presence of Lord Donegall and his father-in-law, Edward May, as captains show that aristocratic influence was not absent, though against this it has to be said that the captaincy of a yeomanry corps was frequently nominal and honorific, particularly outside periods of danger.[132]

These qualifications notwithstanding, viewed in this wider context there are sufficient similarities between Belfast's Volunteers and yeomen with voluntary military organisations in other growing towns at least to merit further investigation. Perhaps such a study would reveal that far from being 'double traitors', the voluntary participation in these organisations was as much part of the social and economic fabric of the growing town and its sense of civic pride as other examples of voluntary endeavour such as the Belfast Chamber of Commerce, the Belfast Charitable Society, the Academical Institution and the Belfast Museum.

NOTES

1   Lane to Downshire, 15 June 1798, PRONI Downshire Papers, D607/F/245.
2   A.T.Q. STEWART, *The Summer Soldiers*, [hereafter: STEWART, *Summer Soldiers*] (Belfast: Blackstaff Press, 1995) pp. 108–9.
3   Author's note: a government raised part-time home defence force started in October 1796. It was officered by local landlords, professional or business people. Yeomanry corps of cavalry and infantry, averaging 50 and 100 respectively, were established in every Irish county and in most towns and cities. See A.F. BLACKSTOCK, *An Ascendancy Army, the Irish Yeomanry, 1796–1832* [hereafter: BLACKSTOCK, *Ascendancy Army*] (Dublin: Four Courts Press, 1998).
4   C.H. TEELING, *Personal Narrative of the 'Irish Rebellion' of 1798*, (London, 1828) pp. 207–8.
5   See D.W. MILLER, 'Non-Professional Soldiery' in T. BARTLETT and K. JEFFERY (eds.) *A Military History of Ireland* (Cambridge: Cambridge University Press, 1996) pp. 315–334.
6   A.T.Q. STEWART, *A Deeper Silence: the Hidden Origins of the United Irishmen*, [hereafter: STEWART, *A Deeper Silence*] (London: Faber and Faber, 1993) p. 19.
7   W.E.H. LECKY, *A History of Ireland in the Eighteenth Century*, [hereafter: LECKY, *Ireland*] (5 vols., London: Longmans, Green & Co., 1913) ii, pp. 394–7.
8   P.D.H. SMYTH, 'The Volunteers, 1778–84', PRONI Document Pack, (Belfast, 1974); P. ROGERS, *The Irish Volunteers and Catholic Emancipation*, [hereafter: ROGERS, *Irish Volunteers*] (London: Burns, Oates and Washbourne, 1934) p. 45.
9   Linen Hall Library, Joy MSS, Vol. 5, p.45.
10 P.D.H. SMYTH, 'The Volunteers and Parliament, 1779–84' in T. BARTLETT and D.W. HAYTON (eds.) *Penal Era and Golden Age: Essays in Irish History, 1690–1800*, [hereafter, BARTLETT and HAYTON, *Penal Era and Golden Age*] (Belfast: Ulster Historical Foundation, 1979) pp. 113–136.
11 T. BARTLETT, *The Fall and Rise of the Irish Nation*, [hereafter: BARTLETT, *Fall and Rise*] (Dublin: Gill and Macmillan, 1992) p. 101.
12 I. MCBRIDE, *Scripture Politics: Ulster Presbyterians and Irish Radicalism in the Late Eighteenth Century*, [hereafter MCBRIDE, *Scripture Politics*] (Oxford: Clarendon Press, 1998) pp. 141–2.
13 STEWART, *Deeper Silence*, p. 50.
14 MCBRIDE, *Scripture Politics*, p. 142; J.E. DOHERTY and D.J. HICKEY (eds.) *A Chronology of Irish History*, (Dublin: Gill and Macmillan, 1989) p. 88.
15 LECKY, *Ireland*, ii, pp. 369–70.
16 Ibid. ii, pp. 394–7.
17 J. KELLY, 'Select Documents XLIII: A secret return of the Volunteers of Ireland in 1784', *Irish Historical Studies*, [hereafter: *IHS*] xxvi, no. 103 (May, 1989), pp. 268–293.
18 J. KELLY, *Prelude to Union: Anglo-Irish Politics in the 1780s*, (Cork: Cork University Press, 1992) pp. 184–5.

19 STEWART, *A Deeper Silence*, p. 164.
20 M. ELLIOTT, *Wolfe Tone: Prophet of Irish Independence*, [hereafter: ELLIOTT, *Wolfe Tone*] (London and Newhaven: Yale University Press, 1989) p. 119.
21 STEWART, *A Deeper Silence*, pp. 138–9.
22 W. WORDSWORTH, *The Prelude*, book xi, lines 108–9.
23 ELLIOTT, *Wolfe Tone*, p. 85.
24 STEWART, *A Deeper Silence*, pp. 112–3; MCBRIDE, *Scripture Politics*, p. 167.
25 MCBRIDE, *Scripture Politics*, pp. 167–8.
26 STEWART, *A Deeper Silence*, pp. 146–7.
27 Haliday to Charlemont, 16 June 1791, *The Manuscripts and Correspondence of James, first Earl of Charlemont*, [hereafter: HMC *Charlemont*] (2 vols., London: Historical Manuscripts Commission, 1891–94) ii, p. 140.
28 CURTIN, *The United Irishmen: Popular Politics in Ulster and Dublin, 1791–1798*, [hereafter: CURTIN: *United Irishmen*] (Oxford: Clarendon Press, 1994) pp. 43–5.
29 STEWART, *A Deeper Silence*, pp. 144–51.
30 Resolutions of the Down Volunteers, 18 Nov. 1792, PRONI Perceval-Maxwell Papers, T1023/138.
31 *Northern Star*, 8–12 Dec. 1792.
32 W. BRUCE and H. JOY (eds), *Belfast Politics*, (Belfast, 1794), pp. 85–7.
33 STEWART, *A Deeper Silence*, p. 183.
34 M. ELLIOTT, *Partners in Revolution: The United Irishmen and France*, [hereafter: ELLIOTT, *Partners in Revolution*] (London and Newhaven: Yale University Press, 1982) p. 35; Curtin, *The United Irishmen*, p. 52.
35 CURTIN, *The United Irishmen*, p. 51.
36 ELLIOTT, *Partners in Revolution*, pp. 57–60; S. TILLYARD, *Citizen Lord: Edward Fitzgerald, 1763–1798*, [hereafter: TILLYARD, *Citizen Lord*] (London: Chatto and Windus, 1997) pp. 153–4.
37 *Northern Star*, 5 Dec. 1792.
38 CURTIN, *The United Irishmen*, p. 52.
39 MCBRIDE, *Scripture Politics*, p. 175.
40 Ibid., p. 175.
41 TILLYARD, *Citizen Lord*, p. 154; Drennan to M. McTier, 25 Nov. 1792, D.A. CHART (ed.) *The Drennan Letters*, [hereafter: CHART (ed.) *The Drennan Letters*] (Belfast, HMSO, 1931), p. 98.
42 Anon to Cooke, 3 Dec. 1792, NAI RP620/19/116.
43 This resulted in his trial two years later for seditious libel, an ordeal which precipitated his withdrawal from active United Irish involvement, see J. LARKIN (ed.), *The Trial of William Drennan* (Dublin: Irish Academic Press, 1991).
44 MCBRIDE, *Scripture Politics*, p. 175.
45 N. CURTIN, 'The transformation of the Society of United Irishmen into a mass-based revolutionary organisation, 1794–6', *IHS*, xxix (May, 1985), pp. 463–92.
46 *Northern Star*, 14–19 March 1796; 20–24 June 1796.
47 Author's note: a proletarian Catholic secret society which grew out of religious disturbances in Armagh, ongoing at different levels of intensity since the 1780s, and which had seen the formation of the Orange Order in 1795 after a particularly severe clash with Defenders known as 'The Battle of the Diamond'.
48 Camden to Pelham, 3 Oct. 1795, British Library [hereafter: BL] Pelham Papers, add mss 33101, f. 306.

49   *Northern Star*, 2–5 Sept. 1796.
50   Author's note: an Irish militia was raised in 1793 including, for the first time in the eighteenth century, Catholic soldiers in the ranks. There was a wide belief that it contained many sworn Defenders and United Irishmen but, despite the discovery and brutal suppression of disaffection in the Monaghan regiment, events in 1798 were to prove these fears much exaggerated. See SIR HENRY McANALLY, *The Irish Militia, 1793–1816*, (Dublin: Clonmore and Reynolds, 1949).
51   For a full discussion see: P.C. STODDART 'Counter-Insurgency and Defence in Ireland, 1790–1805' (unpublished D. Phil. thesis, Oxford University, 1972) chapter 1.
52   J. GOOCH, *Armies in Europe* (London: Routledge and Kegan Paul, 1980) p. 27.
53   W. RICHARDSON, *A History of the Origins of the Irish Yeomanry*, (Dublin, 1801), p. 15.
54   BLACKSTOCK, *Ascendancy Army*, chapter 4.
55   Pelham to Portland, 16 Sept. 1796, Public Record Office, London, Home Office [hereafter PRO (L) HO] 100/66/f. 106.
56   Charlemont to Haliday, 12 Sept. 1796, HMC *Charlemont*, ii, pp. 283–4.
57   Resolutions of the Cookstown Company of the Killymoon Volunteers, 14 Nov. [1796], PRONI Stewart of Killymoon Papers, D3167/2/127.
58   Reverend W. Richardson to Arthur Wolfe, 26 Sept. 1796, NAI RP620/25/118.
59   Handbills n.d. [c. 8–9 Nov. 1796] NAI RP620/26/32.
60   Richardson to Wolfe, 26 Sept. 1796, NAI RP620/25/118.
61   Enclosed in T. Knox to Cooke, 21 Dec. 1796, NAI RP620/26/43.
62   Newtownards Yeomanry Resolutions, n.d. November 1796, PRONI D1494/2/24.
63   Downshire to Cooke, 17 Jan. 1797, NAI RP620/28/109. The feeling was mutual: Martha McTier, one of the voices of radical Belfast, described Downshire's appearance as 'looking like the devil', M. McTier to William Drennan, 17 Mar. 1797, Chart (ed.) *The Drennan Letters*, pp. 252–3.
64   Charlemont to Haliday, 12 Sept. 1796, HMC *Charlemont*, ii, pp. 283–4.
65   McTier to Drennan, 16 Sept. 1796, Chart (ed.) *The Drennan Letters*, pp. 240–1.
66   McTier to Drennan, 25 Sept. 1796, ibid., p. 242; Haliday to Charlemont, 21 Sept. 1796, HMC *Charlemont*, ii, p. 284.
67   Charlemont to Haliday, 12 Sept. 1796, HMC *Charlemont*, ii, pp. 283–4.
68   M. McNEILL, *The Life and Times of Mary Ann McCracken, 1770–1866*, [hereafter: McNEILL, *Mary Ann McCracken*] (Dublin: Allen Figgis and Co., 1960) pp. 73–4.
69   Petition of the distressed loyalists of Belfast to the Marquis of Downshire, 10 Oct. 1796. NAI RP620/25/159.
70   M. HARRISON, *Crowds in History: Mass Phenomena in English Towns, 1790–1835*, (Cambridge: Cambridge University Press, 1988), p. 41.
71   Author's note: a county or a district of a county could be 'proclaimed' out of the King's peace, if a quorum of its magistrates agreed it was 'disturbed' and requisitioned the Castle. Amongst its more notorious provisions were curfews, arms raids and arrests on suspicion.
72   Author's note: it is worth noting that Charlemont opposed the introduction of the Insurrection Act in Armagh and got his way in the face of the county Governor, Lord Gosford's wish for proclamation. Charlemont succeeded

because he threatened to resign from the yeomanry.

73 Portland to Camden, 5 Nov. 1796, PRO (L) HO100/62/f. 321.

74 H. JOY, *Historical Collections Relative to the Town of Belfast*, [hereafter: JOY, *Historical Collections*] (Belfast, 1817), p. 453.

75 Cooke to [?Lake], n.d. [late] December 1796, NAI RP620/26/178.

76 JOY, *Historical Collections*, pp. 450–7; S. MCSKIMIN, *The Annals of Ulster*, [hereafter: MCSKIMIN, *Annals of Ulster*] (Belfast: J. Cleland, 1906), pp. 40–43. See also: *The Memoirs of William Sampson* (New York, 1807) p. 398 (in F.J. Biggar Collection, Belfast Central Library).

77 See also: Pelham to Chichester Skeffington, 4 Jan. 1797, PRONI Foster-Massereene Papers, D562/301.

78 ANON, *To the Inhabitants of Belfast by a Townsman*, (Belfast, 1797) Royal Irish Academy [hereafter: RIA], Haliday Pamphlets, 730/7.

79 MCSKIMIN, *Annals of Ulster*, pp. 40–43.

80 McTier to Drennan, 2 Jan. 1797, CHART (ed.) *The Drennan Letters*, pp. 246–7.

81 Author's note: the 'potato digging' was a novel and effective propaganda device. When a United leader was arrested, hundreds of people would turn out, sometimes marching in military order, to raise the man's crops. The intention was to embarrass the authorities by demonstrating that, despite arrests, large numbers could still be mobilised, yet the 'diggers' stayed within the letter of the law as they could claim they were agricultural workers who only carried spades.

82 Drennan to McTier, 14 Jan. 1797, CHART (ed.), *The Drennan Letters*, p. 247.

83 Skeffington to Pelham, 2, 4 Jan. 1797, NAI RP620/28/14c, 620/28/33 2; Pelham to Skeffington, 4 Jan. 1797, PRONI, Foster-Massereene Papers, D562/301.

84 JOY, *Historical collections*, pp. 451–4; MCSKIMIN, *The Annals of Ulster*, p. 41.

85 MCSKIMIN, *The Annals of Ulster*, p. 42.

86 MCSKIMIN, *The Annals of Ulster*, pp. 42–3.

87 JOY, *Historical Collections*, p. 455; MCSKIMIN, *The Annals of Ulster*, p. 44.

88 ANON, *To the Inhabitants of Belfast by a Townsman*, (Belfast, 1797), RIA Haliday Pamphlets, 730/7.

89 MCSKIMIN, *The Annals of Ulster*, p. 41.

90 Colonel Barber to Cooke, n.d. January 1797, NAI RP620/28/17; 620/28/84; Lake to General J. Knox, 12 Jan. 1797, National Library of Ireland, [here after: NLI] Lake Mss. MS56/f.20.

91 Cooke to ?Lake, n.d. [late] December 1796, NAI RP620/26/178.

92 Colonel Barber to Edward Cooke, n.d. Jan. 1797, NAI RP 620/28/17, 84; see also: General Lake to General Knox, 12 January 1797, NLI Lake Papers, MS56/f.20.

93 *Freeman's Journal*, 17 Sept.; 1 Oct. 1796.

94 JOY, *Historical Collections*, p. 452.

95 ANON, *A Handbill Lately Circulated from the Belfast Post Office and Cool Strictures Thereon by an Irishman*, (Dublin, 1797) pp. 10–12; ANON, *To the Inhabitants of Belfast by a Townsman*, (Belfast, 1797) pp. 6–7, RIA Haliday pamphlets 730/7. For partial transcripts see: JOY, *Historical Collections*, pp. 445–6.

96 Charlemont to Haliday, 1 February 1797, HMC *Charlemont*, ii, pp. 294–5.

97 *Northern Star*, 13–16 Jan. 1797; *Belfast News-Letter*, 3–6 Jan. 1797.

98 McTier to Drennan, 13, 30, 30 Jan. 1797, CHART (ed.) *The Drennan Letters*, pp. 248–9.

99   Camden to Downshire, 4 Jan. 1797, PRONI Downshire Papers, D607/E/7.

100 McTier to Drennan, 30 Jan. 1797, CHART (ed.) *The Drennan Letters*,
     pp. 248–9.

101 There were 27 privates; for their names see JOY, *Historical Collections*, p. 461.

102 JOY and BRUCE, *Belfast Politics*, pp. 98-107; J. GRAY, 'A tale of two news
     papers: the contest between the *Belfast News Letter* and the *Northern Star* in
     the 1790s' in J. GRAY and W. McCANN (eds.) *An Uncommon Bookman*,
     (Belfast: Linen Hall Library, 1996), p. 178.

103 Downshire to Cooke, 17 Jan. 1797, NAI RP620/28/109. He was replaced as
     captain by Rainey, but joined the Belfast Infantry as a non-operative
     member, giving money to funds for those injured in the fighting in 1798.
     JOY, *Historical Collections*, pp. 451–4.

104 Lake to Knox, 12 Jan 1797, NLI Lake Mss, MS56/f.20.

105 Rankin to Pelham, n.d. Jan. 1797, NAI RP620/28/72.

106 *The Dublin Gazette*, 19–21 Jan. 1797, p. 41; 9–11 Feb. 1797, p. 100;
     2–4 April 1797, p. 222.

107 H.M. WHITE to C.S. STEPHENSON, Washington, USA, n.d. Feb. 1797,
     NAI RP620/28/276.

108 'Portrait of a soldier yeoman', enclosure in T. Whinnery to J. Lees, 10 Feb.
     1797, NAI RP620/28/249.

109 J. LAWLESS, *Belfast Politics Enlarged*, (Belfast, 1818), p. 5.

110 O. MACDONAGH, *O'Connell: the Life of Daniel O'Connell, 1775–1847*,
     [hereafter MACDONAGH, *O'Connell*] (London: Weidenfield and Nicolson,
     1991) p. 55.

111 L.H.L. JOY Mss. Vol. 5.

112 MACDONAGH, *O'Connell:*, p. 258.

113 Membership card for 'The Volunteers of 1782 Revived' branch of the repeal
     Movement, NLI; see cover illustration of D.G. BOYCE, *Nationalism in Ireland*
     (Baltimore: Johns Hopkins University Press, 1982).

114 P. O'SNODAIGH, *The Irish Volunteers, a list of the Units, 1715–93* (Dublin:
     Four Courts Press, 1995).

115 G. Knox to Lord Abercorn, 14 Feb. 1793, PRONI Abercorn Papers,
     T2541/1B1/4/12.

116 McNEILL, *Mary Ann McCracken*, p. 140.

117 McTier to Drennan, 17 March 1797, CHART, *The Drennan Letters*, p. 252
see also M.A. McCracken to H.J. McCracken, 16 March 1797, Trinity College
     Dublin, Madden Papers, MS873.

118 Cited in Stewart, *A Deeper Silence*, p. 20.

119 P.D.H. SMYTH, 'The Volunteers and Parliament' in BARTLETT and HAYTON
     (eds.) *Penal Era and Golden Age*, pp. 114–5, 121.

120 The recollections of Morgan Jellett, [c. 1830], PRONI T2777/A.

121 Resolutions of the Belfast Cavalry, 6 May 1808, PRONI D395/2.

122 A Prince of the House of Orange who ruled over the Republic of the United
     Provinces, as the Netherlands were known until 1795.

123 S. SCHAMA, *Patriots and Liberators: Revolution in the Netherlands, 1780–1813*,
     (London: Collins, 1977) pp. 87–8, 94.

124 J.E. COOKSON, 'The English Volunteer Movement of the French Wars,
     1793–1815: some contexts', *The Historical Journal*, 32, 4, (1989),
     pp. 867–91.

125 J.E. COOKSON, *The British Armed Nation*, (Oxford: Clarendon Press, 1997)
     p. 10.

126 Haliday to Charlemont, 1 Feb. 1797, HMC *Charlemont*, ii, pp.294–5.

127 Resolutions of the Belfast Cavalry, 6 May 1808, PRONI D395/2.
128 The recollections of Morgan Jellett, [c. 1830], PRONI T2777/A.
129 A. CROSSLEY, 'Brief directions for the conduct of the captains, subalterns and sergeants of yeomanry corps…', (Belfast, 1803), LHL BPB1803.1.
130 Records of the Belfast yeomanry, 4 Oct. 1803, PRONI D3221/1/89.
131 Records of the Belfast yeomanry, 1804–5, PRONI D3221/1/89.
132 A list of the counties of Ireland and their respective yeomanry corps … , 1 June 1798, NLI IR355a4.